WOUNDED
Struck Down But Not Destroyed

Lyla Netmier

Copyright © 2011 by Lyla Netmeir

Wounded
Struck Down But Not Destroyed
by Lyla Netmeir

Printed in the United States of America

ISBN 9781613798515

All rights reserved solely by the author. The author guarantees all contents are original and do not infringe upon the legal rights of any other person or work. No part of this book may be reproduced in any form without the permission of the author. The views expressed in this book are not necessarily those of the publisher.

Unless otherwise indicated, Bible quotations are taken from The Holy Bible New International Version®. Copyright © 1973, 1978, 1984 by International Bible Society.

www.xulonpress.com

Table of Contents

Introduction vii
Acknowledgements
Chapter 1
Beginnings.. 11
Chapter 2
Betrayal 17
Chapter 3
Forgiveness 29
Chapter 4
A Relationship Blossoms 46
Chapter 5
Questions.. 54
Chapter 6
Struggles and Freedoms 66
Chapter 7
Hope for Tomorrow 80

INTRODUCTION

As I sit here watching my husband and my 2 babies play the guitar together, I find it very hard to express what it is that I am trying to say. It's difficult for me to write down words that have never been spoken before. My thoughts scurry and I feel myself stuttering in my mind, but I am determined to someday, soon, tell the world my story.

I know we all find it so hard to forget painful and hurtful things that come at us in life – AND let me tell you, about HALF of my life was made up of just that: anger, hurt, resentment, pain, but most of all, **betrayal**.

This is not just an everyday random story someone thought up. Not. At. All. This is an ongoing story about how there is a BIG Being out there (bigger than all our hurts and all our pain) who took a scared, fragile, bitter little girl from a world of darkness and sorrow into a world of joy and light.

THIS IS MY TESTIMONY

Before I begin I just want to clarify that due to the coarse nature of things that will be said and written (things you will soon discover), I am choosing not to name REAL names or locations.

DEDICATION

I do want to dedicate this first and foremost to my God, the very Being that made this story even possible. He is my inspiration and my very Best Friend.

I also dedicate this to the most amazing man I have ever met: my husband. I would have never found the courage to do this if it weren't for you pushing me and encouraging me with everything in you. You are my hero and I couldn't have asked God for anything more than you. Just You.

Most importantly, I dedicate this to any and every person out there who has ever gone through a related type of pain and hurt. Know that God is with you, and though you may have been struck down, you can never be destroyed.

CHAPTER 1

Beginnings

I remember growing up in a very small town in the countryside. Literally, it was out in the middle of nowhere but it was actually a lot of fun. It was a safe neighborhood where you knew everyone who lived within a 5-mile radius of you, allowing for us to stay connected to everyone and everything around us. It was a blast.

My family was pretty big compared to all our friends and neighbors. I come from a family of 7, and let me tell you, a big family was very hard to find in an area like ours. People were always intrigued and seemed to always ask my parents how they handled having 5 kids on their own while trying to juggle work and marriage along with us. I swear the entire world outside of our home thought we were the perfect family. My parents would always get comments and praise at our "outstanding" behavior inside and out of our home. But even though we may have seemed perfect, my siblings and I, we made up such a crazy and dynamic bunch.

Out of the five of us, I'm what some would call the "motherly" sibling. I was always the one to be left in charge of everything while my parents were out. I had to deal with trying to mediate fights, defend, discipline, and even cook some days. I was always more like my mom. She was (and still is) such an amazing woman in retrospect, especially with all she had on her plate, and I'm not just talking about having 5 kids to deal with.

You see, my dad was raised by an incredibly abusive father, to say the least, and he was brutally beaten almost everyday until he was 15. Later he was drafted by the military in a foreign country. While he was at war, he managed to escape and didn't return to his hometown until he was 20 or so. When he was almost 30 he met my mother and they eloped. A year later they would have their first baby, and about 7 years after that, they would have their last.

Just like any family we had our good days and bad days. Throughout our childhood years my dad was verbally and physically abusive, and I know his upbringing had a lot to do with it. I remember the littlest things would make him snap sometimes and my mom would be the one to have to deal with it. It wasn't like this everyday, but I'm pretty sure the reason we were so well "behaved" was because we were so scared of what his reaction would be or what he would do if we would even consider misbehaving.

Growing up, like every girl, I craved to be loved by my dad. I always desired that affection that every little girl desires, and for so long I tried so hard to get it. But it never *really* came. On one occasion I remember my dad had been really sick for a few days. He had been in bed for an entire week and his condition got really bad one night. I remember him calling us into his room with tears running down his face. He made us sit down at the side of the bed and apologized to each one of us separately. He repeated over and over how sorry he was and how much he didn't want to hurt us like his dad had hurt him. At the end, I remember it so well because it was one of those moments you can never forget, he took me in his arms and embraced me and told me the three words I had been dying to hear: "I love you". I remember we all sobbed together, and for the first time ever we all felt loved by our dad.

From that point, I thought my dad would really change, but he eventually began to feel better and was back to his normal self. It took about a month before the abusive behavior came back... but it did.

As a little girl I remember feeling so confused about everything. My parents raised us in a Christian home where we would go to church. We learned about God and Jesus and the Bible, but I could never understand how God, who supposedly "loved" me, allowed so many horrible things to happen, and not just to me, but to a lot of other people.

When I was a little older (maybe 8 or 9) I began to actually see "things" happen. My mom was a devout Christian. She loved the Lord so much and she was always positive no matter how bad things would get. I remember us not having money to eat some days and out of nowhere food would show up or money would appear. I wondered and thought that maybe, just maybe, there really was something bigger than me out there. And so, I put it to the test.

Before I tell you how I tested my mom's beliefs I think it's important for you to understand that outside of my "motherly" traits, my personality isn't very outgoing. I am probably the exact opposite. I have always been painfully shy, very timid, and quiet. In school I was always "the quiet girl" and would avoid speaking in public more than ANYTHING (and I still do). I still had my handful of friends, but even so, I hated any type of schoolwork that required me to stand in front of my class and have a crowd of faces looking right at me.

Anyways, I was in my 4th grade class and I remember we were given a book report assignment that would require a lot of time. We would have to do presentations in front of the whole class, but the worse part, for me, was that we would have to have a partner. I only had one really good friend in my class and so I whispered a prayer and said: "God, if you really exist, please let Mrs. Johnson choose Becky for my partner." I remember the instant I finished praying that prayer she said, "Lyla you are with Becky." I was shocked and I remember running home very excited to tell my mom. She smiled really big at me when I told her and she told me how happy she was that I had come to the realization that God really did exist. Looking back I know it wasn't just a coincidence. I know God made Himself real to me that day in that "small" and "silly" little way for a reason. That day has stuck with me even till today.

 Things were pretty "normal" through 5th grade and up until the end of my 6th grade school year. But, like a turbulent day, dark and stormy clouds would roll in my way. Satan would soon set off an attack against me that would bring me to the darkest days of my life. It would be the most hurtful betrayal a little girl could encounter.

CHAPTER 2

Betrayal

I personally don't like bad memories, but a memory like this is hard to forget. I remember my siblings and I were all sitting down about to watch TV. We were about to watch Sleeping Beauty for the first time, and about 10 minutes into the movie I suddenly felt something touching me. I don't feel comfortable giving full details, but I would like for those who haven't been through something like this, to understand someone who has. I remember being so scared. When I looked over, to see who or what it was, I saw... it was my very own father.

I remember feeling sick to my stomach, so confused as to what was happening. He looked at me and said, "Do you like that?" I think I went into a moment of shock and so I tried to get up but he would not let me. I was forced to sit there for about an hour while my very own father sexually molested me in front of my siblings. We were under a blanket on the couch, my mom was not home, and the rest of my siblings were all sitting on the floor. Once I was finally able to get up he looked at me and hushed – hinting that I couldn't or shouldn't say anything – like it was a secret. I ran to my room and just sat there feeling extremely confused. I felt frozen and numb while my siblings played around me.

Unfortunately, this wouldn't be the last time it would happen. This went on for almost 2 months, and every time it would happen my mom would be out and we would be watching TV. I was 11 years old and I began to feel extremely terrified of my own father. I was so scared of that man it kept me quiet. What was worse is that my mom would always sit us down and talk to us about personal boundaries, and how we should never allow anyone to touch our bodies inappropriately. She would always make sure to tell us that if it ever happened, we should tell her or my dad immediately.

I felt so confused. How could I tell the person that was molesting me that I was being molested? I felt trapped and scared, so I remained quiet, but as the days, weeks and months went by I began to emotionally and spiritually die inside. I literally felt numb when I was touched by anyone, even when I was being talked to. Sometimes I would find myself not responding, not because I didn't want to, but because words wouldn't come. I remember my siblings asking me why I was being so "weird." I would ignore it all and merely stare out into space or sometimes I would blow up at them and tell them to leave me alone.

Things would just get worse in the coming weeks. My parents told us that we were going to be moving to a bigger city where we would be able to be with more family than where we were living. I loved my home and I really didn't want to leave, but like every child, I didn't really have a say on the decision. One good thing that came out of it was that my parents became so busy with the move that we (my siblings and I) were sort of ignored most of the time. We would be told to sit down and watch movies or play in the basement, which is where we spent most of our time those last few weeks. I hated the thought of moving but it felt good to not have worry about being molested, especially when my mom was home everyday for about a month.

The move was pretty fast and easy. I remember saying goodbye to my home and feeling as if maybe the move would put an end to the dark secret I was carrying around. We moved in with family while we looked for a house, and the first couple of weeks worked out to be very much fun. Even though we all had to sleep in the living room, it all worked out well, and I felt safe at night knowing that my mom was in the same room with me. I knew she wouldn't allow me to get hurt.

Things were going great, until my mom got a job... before my dad. Fear ran up and down my entire being. I knew this wasn't going to be good, and I was right.

On my mom's first week of work my dad took me up to a room and the molestation turned into rape. My father, the person who was supposed to protect me and love me and be there for me, betrayed me in the worst possible way a daughter can be betrayed.

I remember I wasn't allowed to cry and he made me say and do things that I still can't believe I was forced to do. After he raped me, he told me that he was so sorry and that I shouldn't tell anyone what had just happened. He told me that if I told my mom, I would ruin our family and she would be very hurt. In my heart, my mom was my... everything. I loved her so much that the last thing I ever wanted to do was to break her heart. And so, in *my* heart, I chose to not tell a soul. I remembered right after I was raped my dad took my sisters and me to have a play date with some friends. Of course I didn't want to go, but I had to. I remember wanting to cry with everything inside of me, but instead, having to bottle it all up in my small, broken heart because I was so scared.

Writing this is hard for me. It brings tears and hurt. It's a type of pain that is so hard to forget, but it's something that so many girls, and even boys, have been through. It may not be the exact same story, but the pain remains the same.

I wish that were it. I wish I could tell you that that was the last time I was molested or abused, but it wasn't. Even though my dad finally found a job, it did not stop him from hurting me time after time after time. He raped me almost every day before he found a job, and then about 3 times a week on average after that.

We eventually found a house, and though I thought things would get better, I was very wrong again. I fell into such a deep depression. I could no longer hide my darkness. It was written all over my face, but everyone thought it was the move. My parents would tell everyone that they thought I was homesick. My siblings and my friends would constantly ask me what was wrong and instead of teasing or making fun of me, I think they truly began to worry about me.

Of course I would make up some excuse and eventually they would go away, but everyone began to notice that something was wrong. This lead to my dad having a talk with me, except for my mom was with him. He told me to stop acting like a party pooper, to start acting my age, and play the way a child my age should play. My mom was concerned but

I think she thought it was because I was shy and quiet that I was becoming so antisocial.

I began to hide all of my feelings. I didn't want my mom to find out and so I forced myself to become someone else. I forced myself to play and have fun – I even forced myself to like my dad around my family. I would pretend to play with him and laugh with him so I wouldn't be noticed. That seemed to fix most of the concerns my family had over me, but it didn't fix anything inside of me In fact, it even made things worse. But soon school would start and I would have more things to focus on other than what was going on at home.

August came and school started. At first it was very hard, especially because of my personality. I was still the quiet girl, but I began to be sought after by a boy who, unfortunately, was related to me. I was still so confused - I was only 12 and I was craving love and protection more than anything from anyone or anywhere. I watched how girls who dressed a certain way would get more attention from guys and I envied them so much. I wanted love more than anything and so I began to dress extremely promiscuously to get it.

I will not name names, but I began to "fall" for that family member who was almost 3 years older than me that was pursuing me in school. I knew it was wrong but I always questioned if my dad raping me wasn't wrong, why was being with a relative, who I thought really loved me, wrong? I chose to be "loved" by him. He knew his way with words, but at the end of the day, *all* he wanted was the one thing that every boy in high school wants – sex.

I would find every excuse not to go to his house, but finally I gave in. I really thought that he loved me for real. I felt that no matter how wrong it was he was going to protect me and take me away from the hell I was living in. Fortunately, his dad walked in before he was able to completely pressure me into having sex. I was able to hide, and when his dad left I ran out.

We had been together about a total of 6 months and finally I realized that sex was all he *really* wanted from me. I finally said I was done, and the day after, as I walked into school, about 3 boys asked me to be their girlfriend. Because I was impeccably immature and because I was seeking love more than anything, I thought it was the greatest day of my life... until... I found out that my relative, who had said he loved me, spread a horrible rumor about me. He had told all of his friends that I was "easy" and that I would do anything for sex. I instantly became the most sought out girl by every boy and the most hated girl by every other girl in school. It was, thankfully, my last 2 weeks of school, but I became so isolated and avoided looking at anyone who crossed my path. It hurt me so bad to know that all I was wanted or "needed" for was *just* sex. They didn't care about me. They didn't love me for who I was. All they saw was a piece of meat.

    Everything hit me like a ton of bricks and my depression began to worsen. That summer turned out to be very lazy and unproductive for me, which didn't do me any good. I had too much time to think. Of course I would hide it from the world, but I began to have suicidal thoughts. I remember the *one-day* I tried to throw myself out the window, the window got jammed. I then tried to cut myself with a razor blade so I could somehow bleed to death, but one of my siblings walked in.

I finally found something that would keep me busy. We were told we were going to be moving and I was put in charge of boxing. About a month later we moved into a house about 30 minutes away. I was so relieved to get away from everything. I knew horrible things would have waited for me at the start of the next school year had we stayed. Thankfully, I ended up at a school where I could start fresh and nobody knew me. I had a clean slate.

I told myself if I didn't make any friends or make myself stand out with the way I dressed, than I could avoid everything and everyone. And so, even though the rape continued, year after year, I focused on nothing but schoolwork. I got good grades. My teachers loved me and I actually enjoyed school. School was where I could get away. My dad was miles away at work and he couldn't hurt me there and schoolwork was able to entertain me and keep me from thinking about how bad things were at home, except for this *one* week that I clearly remember.

My mom had gone to what she called a retreat. I was so angry. I knew that that week was going to be horrible for me, and I was right. I was raped almost every day, but surprisingly that is actually not what stands out in my memory. I remember at the end of that week when my mom walked through the door she began to cry. She hugged every one of us and told us that God had spoken to her heart about all of us. I was second in line, but I will never forget what she said. She told me that God had told her that He had incredible plans for my life and that I was going to do amazing things. I remember feeling confused and shocked. Incredible plans? ME? Do amazing things? I shook it off my thoughts, but it always kept running through the back of my head.

By the time I got into 10th grade the rape had lessened. We had moved into such a small house that I guess it just became too risky for my dad. The end of that school year would be the last time my dad would rape me.

It was like any other time my dad called me up to his room, as if he were going to ask me a question, at least that's probably what my siblings thought. I went upstairs and he told me to do something he had never told me to do. He asked me to get under the covers. I was so confused. He then undressed himself and had me watch him. Like every other time I began feeling so sick to my stomach. He got under the covers and asked me to "make love to him." He had never told me anything like that. I was so confused. Love? Was this *really* Love?

About two minutes later he got up and told me he was sorry and that he wasn't himself and that it wasn't him. It was as if he had snapped out of it. He gave me back my clothes. I ran out to my room and for the first time I allowed myself to cry and to feel all the pain and the hurt that was bottled up inside. I cried and cried until I couldn't cry anymore. And then I began to feel nothing but hate for my dad. I still wouldn't show the world my feelings, but I know hatred began to take its place in my heart. I no longer felt numb. I had finally let myself feel, but it would unfortunately just make things worse.

CHAPTER 3

Forgiveness

At the end of my 10th grade year we moved...*again*. Stability was not my family's strong point, which I'm sure you probably figured out after about our 3rd move. But it was different this time, mostly because we moved to a very different location, about 1,000 miles away. I remember feeling extremely disheartened. I had really begun to enjoy going to school and I knew I would have to start *all* over. What if I had mean teachers? What if they didn't like me? I was so anxious. Fortunately, we had some family where we moved to and they were able to show us around. Before I knew it, I was actually beginning to really like the new place.

The beginning of the school year rolled around pretty fast and I was very nervous. About 3 weeks in, I had actually made a couple of friends, and to make it better, I really liked my teachers. Life was going pretty well for me. At least, that's what *I* thought. Here I was carrying around this big ball of hatred that was continually growing inside of me and I thought I was fine. Hate had begun to penetrate through my very core and it actually began to feel good.

This hatred that was growing inside my heart began to really affect any interaction I had with any boy. When I looked at any guy, I would see the boy who had used me in middle school and my very own dad who had raped me for 5 years. I hated *all* men. It didn't matter what their age was, I saw them all as evil and disgusting beings. Deep down inside, I was still always very afraid that my dad, or any boy, would try to hurt me again. It didn't matter though. I wouldn't allow anyone to see that because I would always mask my fear with hatred. At times I even tried to convince myself that I really wasn't scared anymore, but deep down inside, I was still the same terrified, little girl who had been robbed of her innocence.

One thing that helped me not to worry so much was that my parents found a job where they worked in the same building. I no longer had to worry about them coming home at different times, and I knew that my mom was going to be there when my dad got home from work. Even still, when my mom would go out for absolutely anything, you better believe that I was right there with her. I felt as though I were her "shadow." My mom and I became very close at this time. I think she always thought that I just wanted to spend more time with her, and as a mother she didn't question it. I'm glad she didn't.

As soon as we had moved, my mom began a long and exhausting search for a church to attend. I began to see her getting desperate. In the back of my head I always wondered why God meant so much to her. My aunt and cousins heard that we were looking for a church and they invited us to attend theirs. It didn't take much. Both my parents decided they liked it and so it became our own church.

We fit in pretty well almost immediately, at least everyone else did, but it was good to finally start making mutual friends with my siblings. It helped me to fit in more, I guess, which was a nice change. Don't get me wrong, my siblings and I were always the best of friends, but we never really had any mutual friends until we started attending this particular church.

We began attending youth group services, and before we knew it, we were attending youth events and conventions. Things were going well, I thought, but every time we would attend any youth event they would always do worship and altar calls after sermons (altar calls is when at the end of a service the pastor invites people up front to pray), things that personally I thought were useless. I began to feel nothing more than resentment for God. How could a God who "loved" me have allowed such horrible things to happen to me? How could *my mom* love a God who allowed for her and her kids to be physically and verbally abused by her own husband? I didn't understand, and so on nights like these, the anger and resentment that I felt towards God would just get bigger. I would ignore everything around me: the worship the sermons, everything. I even began to pity those around me who really "thought" that God really loved them.

Spring came about very fast and everyone in our youth group began to feel nothing more than excitement. In about two weeks we would be taking a long road trip to a youth retreat that was expected to be nothing less than pure, unadulterated fun. I remember being excited for reasons no one else was. I would, for the very first time, be far away from my father for more than a week. This was *it* for me. There was nothing more that I could have ever wanted and I couldn't wait.

Those two weeks flew by and I was more than ready to hit the road. My mom came to see us off, and after about what felt like an eternity to make sure we had everything, we were finally on our way. We made some really good time, and after about 3 days of sightseeing, bathroom breaks, and stretching breaks we had arrived.

The campsite was nothing like I thought it would be. I expected a really pretty hotel with big rooms and luxurious bathrooms. Instead, we were situated in cabins that looked more than a century old in the middle of a rainy forest. For someone who wasn't too fond of dreary and gloomy scary places I was *not* happy. Our showers consisted of 90% cold water and cement floors. Our rooms were made up of bunk beads that seemed to squeak if you even drew a breath. The only thing that helped me get through was the food. I must admit it was delicious.

    Our first day there we had to get settled in, have some dinner, and then get ready for our first youth service, which I was not looking forward to. I remember going back to my cabin where a line of about 15 girls stretched all the way outside. I had never seen so many girls desperate to look their best for a "church service" of all things. I still don't know what it is with camps and retreats and girls dying to get a shower *everyday*. I always wonder if they just want to seem like the kind of girl that showers everyday or if they really are hygiene crazy. Anyways, I could have cared less about getting in the shower – I was too tired to stand in a line for 45 minutes just to take a 2-minute ice-cold shower. And so, I lay on my very uncomfortable, squeaky bed and thought about how good it felt to feel so much relief from being away from my dad.

I remember chatting with my sister about how weird it felt to actually be so far from home. We were both so excited. The long trip had allowed for us to really bond. It was nice to have a long conversation about silly stuff for the first time, in a long time, with one of my bestest friends.

30 minutes, 5 bitter, shower-less girls, and a long conversation later, we were moments away from officially launching our retreat. The service began and went on and on... and on. I dozed off too many times to count. I was exhausted and the only thing that kept me busy was looking for anything funny or embarrassing to point out to my sister to make us both laugh.

After what felt like an eternity, we finally dismissed, and I remember being very eager to go to bed and get some long awaited sleep, but those weren't anybody else's plans. It was my first retreat and I wasn't aware that my night was not even close to being over. Some number of events had been planned out for us and we were told that we had to pick at least one thing to do. I was furious. I decided that

I was not going to let them ruin my newly found sense of joy and so I snuck away into my cabin and went to bed.

The next morning I remember waking up feeling good. I was the last one up in my cabin and by the time I actually got up out of bed, the showers were free. I took my time and used up the little bit of hot water that was left. Once I was done, I was off to have some breakfast.

After breakfast, everyone gathered together and we were separated into teams to play some games. It may be hard to believe, but that was my first game of tug-of-war. I had seen it on TV, but had never actually been a part of a tug-of-war. Our team did pretty well, but not good enough to get 1st place. My hands were burning by the time we were all done and I remember the blisters that formed being extremely painful. The day went on, we did a couple more activities and had lunch.

After lunch, we were told to gather up in our rooms to talk to our leaders about what we were getting out of this retreat so far. Of course I remained completely silent, and when it came time for me to share I remember wanting to say "blisters." So far that was all that I had gotten: blisters. I was never the type to get smart, especially with someone older than me, and so I came up with a quick, lame answer and I was done. About 30 minutes later we had reflection time, which consisted of us having "quiet" time to think about God and our lives and that kind of stuff. Fortunately, I wasn't the only who didn't want to reflect, and so we made a plan to pull a prank on the boys.

While the boys were having their dinner, we went into their rooms and put shaving cream on everything. It was probably the most thrilling thing I had ever done. I remember my heart racing so fast as we ran out and back into our cabins. We waited for about two minutes and decided we wanted to see their reaction. We headed back over, waited behind their cabin, and peeked into their window. As they walked in we immediately saw their faces drop and chaos began. We were laughing so hard we could barely run. Unfortunately, someone saw us running and they sent someone to tell us that payback was on its way. I was so nervous that they would do something really bad to my things, and so I hid most of my stuff between my bed and the springs. As silly as it all was, I had never had so much fun. Little did I know that my day was *very* far from over.

We went and had our dinner and before we knew it, it was already time to get ready for service all over again. The shower lines and curling irons were up and running on schedule. 30 minutes later we were off to our 2nd youth service and I was expecting a repeat of the night before. They started off with worship and about half way through I began to feel a knot in my stomach. The songs they were singing were actually having an impact on me, but not as much as the very last song that they sang that night. I remember the chorus so perfectly even today. I have to translate it, but it went something like:

> *Wreck my heart*
> *Wreck my life*
> *I hand my will over to You*
> *All that I am, Lord*
> *All that I have is Yours*
> *I want to decrease*
> *So You can grow in me*

That song, for some reason, resonated in my heart that night. Tears ran down my face. I did my best to hide it from everyone around me. I could feel myself softening up and I began to realize that there really was something bigger than me out there. At that moment I couldn't help but remember that day in my 4th grade class when God had made himself real to me. They finished the song and someone went up to welcome everyone and talk about events and things that would be taking place the next few days. I was in a complete trance. What was happening inside of me? I couldn't focus on anything but that.

Finally the speaker for that night went up and I was shocked to see whom it was. You see, it wasn't just anybody; it was my cabin leader. She was the only person who had tried so hard to encourage me and love me from the time we had got to the camp. She was one of the very few people who I felt genuinely cared for me, and there she was, about to start a sermon. I was all ears. She began talking about her childhood life, and after about 10 minutes, I realized she was going to share her story.

She talked about how she grew up in a poverty stricken town in her country. Her mom passed away early on in her life and her sister was all she had. Unfortunately, her sister was addicted to drugs and had a boyfriend who was a drug addict as well as a gang member. She told us how she would come home some days and find them both completely passed out with needles in their arms. Sometimes there would be 15 to 20 people passed out all around her house. Her sister was always doing drugs, and when she tried to talk to her, all she would get was a cold shoulder.

She didn't have many friends at school because everyone knew about her sister being a drug addict, but one of the friends she did have invited her to church. She began to attend church regularly and gave her life to Jesus. Once her sister found out about her attending church, she forbid her from ever going again. Church was all she had and she was no longer allowed to go. Even so, she would pray and pray that one day she would be able to go again.

One day, as she was in her room, her sister's boyfriend walked in and tried to rape her. Fortunately for her, he was too drugged and she was able to escape. She tried to tell her sister, but of course she didn't listen. And so, she finally decided to run away. When she realized she had no place to go she went to the church where her friend had invited her. Her friend's family took her in and she began to attend church again. Her sister tried to get her back, but she knew that it was too risky to get the police involved due to the fact that she was a drug addict.

Life was great after that day. She was going to church 3 times a week. She made so many friends, and after some years she even met her husband there. They were soon married and had their first baby. Everything was going well, until a few months later when she got very sick and could barely even get up.

Nobody knew what was wrong. She saw so many doctors and tried everything they said, but nothing would ever help. She prayed and prayed and prayed, but nothing would happen. She fell into a deep depression and began to feel angry towards God and also ended any connection she had with Him. After about 6 months, her husband begged her to go to church and so she went. At the end of the service she went up for prayer and the Lord spoke to her through the pastor. He told her God loved her and that He was going to heal her.

She told us that after she had been healed she realized that satan had been attacking her. God knew that she could endure, and she did. God gave her the strength to get through it all and she believed in her heart that she would be healed. After that experience, she began working with the youth and was soon appointed as a youth pastor.

As she finished her sermon, she told us that ever since she had been a youth pastor, she had been through high ups and low downs, but that no matter where she was, God was right there. She knew God was taking care of her when she was little. God had protected her from drugs and from all the horrible things she faced as a child because He knew she would one day lead young people to Christ. I will never forget the words she said as she came to a close: "No matter what you have been through or what you are going through now, if you let God in your heart He can and He will help you."

As she said these words, I began to cry like a little girl. She did an altar call and I could feel my heart beating outside of my chest. I was one of the first to get up because I was so desperate. I began to sob like I had never sobbed before. I asked God to help me as they led us in a sinner's prayer. As soon as we finished that prayer I felt an overwhelming sense of peace, and for the first time in my life, I felt loved like I had never felt loved before. I felt warmth run up and down all of my body and I heard the Lord whisper into my heart: "Lyla, I love you. I have always loved you and I *will* always love you."

I remember falling to the ground and I let myself just cry all of my pains, all of my hurts, and all of the hatred and anger I had bottled up inside. I told God that my dad had raped me and I told him that it hurt me so much. I will never forget what He whispered into my heart. He said, "You have to forgive him Lyla. You can't hold this over his life; your dad loves you."

At that moment, I looked up and I whispered through sobs and tears, "I forgive you daddy." I let myself forgive him and, believe it or not, it only took an instant. I had forgiven my dad, and in that very moment, a huge weight was lifted off of my shoulders.

We began singing praise and worship songs and it seemed like we were there all night just thanking God for what He had done.

That night I was too excited to even think of sleep. God had spoken to me and had made himself so real in my life. Even though I couldn't tell everyone exactly what had just happened, God knew exactly how I felt. My sister could see it and so could all of the girls in my cabin, and thankfully I wasn't the only one. So many of the other girls had walked up to the altar and had their own encounter with God, including my sister, and for that I was so grateful. We were all so excited that night and so we had some good old-fashioned girl talk for about an hour. I don't remember falling asleep, but we all eventually did.

We woke up to a sunny morning and we were more than excited to kick the day off. The rest of the week went by so fast. We had so much fun, and for the rest of the week my favorite part of the day was our youth services. Night after night, I learned more about God and learned what true worship was and how God's love is unconditional.

It was a very sad day when we realized that our week had come to an end. We had a morning mini-service, and we all gathered up for a big group picture. An hour later we were all packed and ready to head back home. I had mixed feelings, but I knew I wasn't the same. We were on the road and it wasn't until half way home that I began to question everything that had just happened.

CHAPTER 4

A Relationship Blossoms

When we were just minutes away from home, I wasn't sure how I felt. I had so many mixed emotions. I was excited, confused, and scared at the same time. What if my dad tried to hurt me again? Why didn't God save *me* from being raped and saved my counselor? Was what I had experienced that past week all made up in my head? So many questions ran in my head as we pulled up to our church parking lot. I put all my questions away in my mind and decided I would think about it later. For now, I was full of excitement to see my mom. I hadn't been that far from her ever and it felt as if I had been gone for months. My siblings and I were so excited to tell stories of the fun and the crazy things that had taken place. She laughed and gazed with tears in her eyes as she realized that God had done something special in each of our lives.

As we pulled up to the driveway, it hit me that this was going to be a terrifying or exciting moment for me. In my head I thought I would see my dad and instantly feel either a sense of fear or love. Sadly, neither happened.

I wish I could say that I ran up to my dad and embraced him in love and forgiveness, but it was not exciting at all. We walked in the door and he was sitting on the couch, as always, watching TV. He looked at us and said his casual "hi" and went back to watching his favorite show. We all said "hi" almost in unison and went back to our rooms to unpack. It was the most anti-climatic moment I had ever experienced, but at least we had come home when he was in a good mood.

We unpacked, had dinner, and I decided to go to my room to think. I sat on my bed and looked out the window. Now I know that at that very moment there was an actual war going on around me between God and satan. I felt as if God was tugging at my heart because I could not stop thinking of his whispers into my heart. But, at the same time, I knew satan was fighting to get my attention as well. I remember feeling so confused and so I decided to pray.

I wasn't big on praying, but in that past week at the retreat, I had prayed more than I had ever prayed my entire life. So I began to ask God to help me get through, at least, the first week I was home. And He did. That week flew by, and I remember going to youth group and feeling as if I had never left our retreat. I realized that I didn't have to be in a far away youth event to have an encounter with God. Week after week, I began to seek the Lord. I began to pray for strength and peace, but more than anything, I prayed for my dad not to hurt me again.

I was new to Christianity and I knew there were things that, as a Christian, would help me to get through life. I remember picking up a Bible for the first time and being a little confused. It wasn't in English, and even though I am bilingual, I understand things better in English. So I went into my little brothers room and found his Children's Bible. The difference to me was amazing, and so I began to read. It may sound silly, but I learned so much from that Children's Bible. It didn't get rid of my fears altogether, but it helped me to know God little by little so I could look past my fear and trust Him for the best.

Time flew by, and before I knew it I had graduated from high school. For financial and many personal issues (including fear) I wasn't able to go to college. I decided to take a year off to get to know the Lord as well as myself. In that year, I remember the Lord showing me bits and pieces of who He was. I read many books, including the Bible, and learned about God and His love and about my journey here on earth. I realized that my life had a purpose. It was always so hard for me to grasp that, but I knew that God had plans for my life. I fell madly in love with God that year. He helped me to get past so much fear that I had bottled up inside, and soon I learned that I could really trust Him. I remember always going to my room just to spend time with Him.

Every time I looked out my window, I could feel God's beauty all around me. I know the scenery helped, and I couldn't help but think that God had put all of the beautiful landscape outside my very window just for me to enjoy. I read a book once about how God knows us inside and out and how He will give us little kisses or signs of love. I, for instance, love looking up at the sky. Everything about it: the sun, the moon, the clouds, the stars, *everything*.

I remember one particular day looking out of my window and seeing a beautiful bird. I think it was an eagle. It was so big and marvelous that it literally took my breath away. I know in my heart that that bird was a kiss from God, a way for Him to remind me that He loves me. I hope you can take that with you wherever you find yourself in life. God loves you and knows what takes *your* breath away.

When I was 18, I remember my mom talking to my sisters and me about boys. I remember still feeling not so much hatred towards men, but bitterness if you may. Even though I didn't hate men, I still saw things at school that made me more resistant towards ever having a boyfriend or even getting married. The main example being that I would see how guys would look at girls as if they were objects of pleasure instead of actual human beings who had feelings. I remember after our conversation I looked at my mom and my sisters and told them that I would never, EVER get married. They thought it was hilarious, of course, but at that moment I was *very* serious.

Naturally, the Lord decided to challenge me with my statement. That year, I met my husband at one of our youth events. I had seen him before, but he was not an actual member of our youth group. He attended another church about 20 minutes away. Anyways, we were having a fundraiser and we were paired to work together. To be honest, he didn't faze me. He was a very funny guy and I didn't think anything of it, until I realized that I was actually comfortable being around him. I was never able to be around a boy without feeling somewhat awkward and here I was enjoying the company of a young man. Not a female, but a MALE.

We became good friends, and about 2 months later I began to have feelings for him. We went on a first date, and after 4 months we began dating. That turned out to be one of the greatest years of my life… and then things got kind of rough again.

That year the Lord gave me a job opportunity that I could not turn down. It stretched me farther than I thought I could be stretched. I was never home and I missed my family. Even though I enjoyed my job, I loved being home more. My siblings were my best friends, and I would barely see them during the week. It was hard, but God knew what He was doing.

A year and a half, and lots of spiritual stretching and growing later, the Lord spoke into my heart again. Believe it or not, the Lord pressed it on my heart to marry the man He had hand picked for me. It was exciting yet confusing. How was I supposed to tell my then boyfriend that God wanted us to get married? I decided that I couldn't just *not* do anything. I gathered up the courage to tell him. I was so scared of what he would say or do, but when I told him what God had put in my heart, I was shocked at his response. All he said was "okay." *Now* he tells me that he was actually shocked and confused, but he also said that he couldn't say no to God.

We decided to pray about everything. We didn't want to rush into something that we weren't 100% sure of. Then, about three weeks later, after lots of praying and seeking for God's will, he proposed. It was one of the most exciting experiences and I will never forget it. About 3 months after the *most* beautiful proposal, we were married. That was the most exciting day of my life, along with the birth of my babies.

    I didn't know that I could be so happy. It still is crazy to me how God can really take a hold of someone's life and turn it all around. I was like a wounded bird that couldn't fly, but God healed me and gave me the strength to soar higher than I could have ever imagined.

CHAPTER 5

Questions

You may be thinking, "Is that it?" "Is that the end?" Not at *all*. Like I said, this is still an ongoing saga. There are definitely things that I still question. I still have doubt and sometimes I still hurt, but God has always been so faithful.

If you have or are going through something similar, I know that you may have one specific question in particular: WHY?

I can't say that what I am about to tell you is going to make it all better, like when a little kid asks their mom to kiss a boo-boo and that's the end of it. It took a lot of time for me to come to a place where I could just let everything go. But it is possible, and I want you to know that.

One particular day, before I was even engaged, I remember that question running through my head over and over again. "Why did my dad rape me?" "If God loves me, why didn't He save me?" "WHY?"

I remember I was at work and the only place I could be alone was in the bathroom. I sat there as those questions kept running through my mind over and over and over again. I began to cry and I began to question *everything* all over again. "How could *You* (God) have allowed for me to be raped by my own father?" After about 5 minutes, this is what God whispered into my heart:

"Your dad didn't rape you Lyla – satan did. Your dad didn't hurt you – satan did. You may think that your dad did this, but satan did it – because satan knew that I had big plans for your life and he tried to ruin those plans. But, he couldn't. He couldn't destroy My plans and he couldn't destroy you. One day you will see - I will turn all the bad into good, I promise."

I was shocked at how clear those words resonated in my heart that day, and at that moment everything became so clear. My dad had said it himself. The last time I was raped he said it wasn't him and that he wasn't himself. It was satan, because satan knew that God had plans for me. He knew that my life had a purpose and *he* was going to do everything in *his* power to prevent me from fulfilling them. And so, he utilized my dad to attack me at my very core.

This may be hard to understand, but I want you to know that satan has power over the earth and he can control people if they don't have Jesus in their hearts. That is how he used my dad. My dad was not seeking God and was allowing the devil to gain control over him.

I was finally able to grasp everything. It was as if all of those questions were a big load that was still weighing on me. As God answered that question that day, it felt like He had physically lifted that load off of me. I hope those words resonate with you as well. I'm not writing this for nothing. I know God whispered that to me because He knew others would need to hear that as well. I urge you, if you can, to just stop and read those words again and again because they were meant for *you* as well.

"[He/She] didn't rape you [place your name] – satan did. [He/She] didn't hurt you – satan did. You may think that [he/she] did this, but satan did it – because satan knew that I had big plans for your life and he tried to ruin those plans. But, he couldn't. He couldn't destroy My plans and he couldn't destroy you. One day you will see - I will turn all the bad into good, I promise."

Now, I know there may be more questions that you have like, "Why didn't God stop it from happening?" I don't know that answer, and to be honest, there are days when I wish that question could be answered both for you and for me. All I can tell you is that we live in a world where satan rules, a world where satan has power to manipulate and to use people to do harm.

Because of the fall of Adam and Eve (read Genesis 2 and 3) there is sin, and because of that very reason, life can't be perfect. Very bad things happen to very good people.

Unfortunately, no one is exempt from being attacked by the devil; not you, not me, not even Jesus himself while he lived on earth. NO ONE.

That may not be what you wanted to hear. I know, because for a long time, I wanted a better answer, but I had to trust God through it. I wish life *were* perfect. I know we all do, but I promise a reward waits for those of us who endure adversity just like Jesus did. *Because* He endured and because He chose to trust God, in spite of all the horrible things He went through, He conquered death and He is the reason we have forgiveness and are able to now have a genuine relationship with God.

Satan will do everything in his power to strike you down over and over until he destroys you. I plead with you today *not* to give up. If you are being attacked, it's because there is something big in store for you that satan is trying to keep you from. I was struck down over and over with rape, with hatred, with fear, with doubt, and with so many other schemes of the devil, but I finally made the decision to take God with me and to trust Him through all the bad.

I'm not saying life will be perfect. What I am saying is that when you ask Jesus to come into your heart, you will experience peace that will go beyond your understanding, power that can move mountains, the most genuine and unconditional love, forgiveness, and so much more. God made us to love us and for us to love Him back, and the devil takes it as his job to try to separate us from Him. But guess what? He can't:

*"Who shall separate us from the love of Christ? Shall **trouble** or **hardship** or persecution or famine or nakedness or danger or sword?*
*No, in all these things we are more than **conquerors** through him who loved us. For I am convinced that neither death nor life, neither angels not demons, neither the present nor the future, nor any powers, neither height nor depth, nor anything else in all creation, will be able to separate us from the love of God that is in Christ Jesus our Lord."*
- *Romans 8:35, 37-39*

If you are going through something difficult, I want you to know that God loves you.

He knows you and He wants to love you more than anything. Just open your heart and let Him in. He said it himself:

"Here I am! I stand at the door and knock. If anyone hears my voice and opens the door, I will come in and eat with him, and he with me." -
Revelation 3:20

I wish I could make that life changing decision for all of you out there, but I can't. It's your own choice to let God in. I know it may seem risky. I've been there. Satan will do everything in his power to keep you from giving your life to God. But why let the very being who has struck you down keep you from fulfilling your purpose in life? Why let him win?

The devil tried so hard to destroy everything in my life. He didn't want me to accomplish any plans that God had for me. But here I am, walking with God, happily married with 2 amazing babies, and, on top of that, I am writing this book. *That* is how God is turning my pain and my hurts into good.

I know, maybe you feel confused, especially if you have never heard about God, the Bible, or salvation. I will give you a quick summary. Maybe a lot of people wouldn't do it this way, but I will try to make it as quick and easy to understand.

God created Adam and Eve and everything was perfect, but the devil tempted Adam and Eve into sin. Since then, there has been sin in the world and the devil has continued to tempt people. As a result, many turned away from God and chose to live a life full of sin. The devil's goal has been, and still is, to turn people away from God.

Now, because of sin, people could not have a relationship with God. Back in the day, people who wanted forgiveness for their sins would have to take an animal to someone else (a priest) who would sacrifice that animal to God on their behalf. Keep in mind that without the blood that was sacrificed, there was *no* forgiveness.

After a very long time, God sent His only son Jesus to earth. Jesus came to earth to be the ultimate sacrifice for our sins. He died on a cross for you and me, and after 3 days, He arose from the dead. Jesus defeated death.

This changed everything. People no longer had to go to someone else with an animal for forgiveness. Because Jesus sacrificed himself for us, we can personally go directly to God. We can ask Him on our own behalf to forgive us for our mistakes, and, on top everything else, we get the privilege to embark on a journey of getting to know who God is for ourselves.

Jesus loved us so much that he gave His life to save us from hell and eternal suffering. Now, we can look forward to a place called Heaven where everything will be perfect. No more suffering. No more hate; just joy, happiness, and perfection. It will be a *true* paradise.

I want to encourage you to read the Bible so you can discover who God is for yourself. If you don't have one, I encourage you to go out and get yourself one. If you don't have the means, the Internet has some great resources or you can find a local church to attend and speak to someone there to help you.

This brings me to another important point: find a local church to attend. It is very important to find a place where you can learn, grow spiritually, and build relationships with others. Church is also a place where

God speaks through people, like my friend who was a youth pastor. God has appointed leaders (pastors) to help guide you and me on this long journey towards Heaven. I don't know what would have happened to me if I didn't have church. I have built relationships with people who have helped me get through so much. God puts people in our lives for a reason and there is nothing more that I want for you than a shoulder to lean on and a friend to trust in when life gets hard; someone who will help encourage you to stay strong and trust that God is always there for you.

You can be a part of God's big plan, if you would just receive that love and forgiveness by asking Jesus to come into your heart. I know life can be so painful and I know that you may have been wounded and hurt to *your* core. I know the feeling, but God wants to heal you. All you have to do is give Him the chance.

Whoever you are and where ever you find yourself today, know that some one out there is praying for you.

So, What are you waiting for? Take a leap of faith. I promise, you will never regret it. Let God in.

"...If you confess with your mouth, "Jesus is Lord," and believe in your heart that God raised him from the dead, you will be saved."
*"As the scripture says, "Anyone who **trusts** in him will **never** be put to shame."*
• *Romans 10:9 & 11*

If you would like to ask Jesus into your heart, here is a prayer that you can pray *out loud*.

Dear Jesus,
I come to you today with a shattered heart. You know what's going on in my life. You know everything about me: my hurts, my pain, and all that I've been through. I want to be free, God. I no longer want to carry this heavy load in my heart. I need You so bad. Please help me.
I know now that You came to earth to save me. You died on a cross and on the 3rd day You rose from the dead so that I could have forgiveness and a genuine relationship with You. Please come into my heart. I believe in You and I want to get to know You more.

*I pray that You would meet me here right where I am. Speak to my heart. In Jesus' name, I pray.
Amen.*

I want to encourage you to take some time right now to pray. Close the book if you have to, find a quiet place, and just tell God how you feel and ask Him to speak to your heart. I hope and pray that you will experience the presence of God and that your life will be changed forever.

CHAPTER 6

Struggles and Freedoms

If you decided to let Jesus into your heart, know that it was the difference between a life of darkness and a life of joy. I am excited for you and I hope you can soon see, with your own eyes, how big God really is. You are going to experience a life full of purpose and meaning.

I do want to let you in on a couple of things, however. Now that you have Jesus in your heart, know that satan will try to rob you of that joy over and over again. Stay strong and trust God. I have seen people whose lives have been transformed by God, and who fall away and turn from Him, all because they begin to believe the lies that satan tells them.

I was so close that day when I came home from my first retreat. I felt like maybe it was all just a lie and that I had somehow made it all up in my head, but I prayed and prayed that God would help me to stay strong. I urge you to do the same.

Just writing this book I have experienced so much chaos in my life. I have come down with the flu, allergies, laziness, impatience, self-doubt, anger, my kids have gotten sick almost every week, and my marriage has been attacked. To be honest, some days I feel so distant from God that I question all the verses in the Bible that say He is near.

Because I started writing this book, satan has attacked me on so many different levels. But, by the grace of God, I'm still alive, and I plan on putting up a fight to finish what I have started. I refuse to let myself be defeated by the very being that struck me down.

In your journey you may experience disheartening days where you just feel discouraged and maybe even depressed. I have struggled with so many different things. Satan has tried to use these things against me, and I will tell you about them so that you don't feel alone if you happen to experience them as well.

MY RELATIONSHIP WITH MY DAD

First, I want to discuss my relationship with my dad. Since the year that I came home from my first youth retreat, I have struggled with trying to build a relationship with my dad. I know my dad noticed a difference when I came home that day. I didn't look at him with hatred, but I didn't look at him with love either. After that day, it has been extremely hard for me to express love to him, both because of fear and because I felt pretty much indifferent about him. He would avoid talking to me if we were ever alone, and I believe it's because he felt so ashamed. I could see it in his eyes. But, I think there was finally a small breakthrough on the day that his mom died.

My mom called me that day to give me the news. I could hear my dad sobbing. He was so torn up, and when I got home, all I could do was cry with him. I held him for so long that day and told him that I loved him. Ever since, his attitude changed toward me and he actually began to show some signs of affection. He helped out with wedding costs and told me he loved me in front of everyone at our wedding reception. I remember on my 22nd birthday he gave me the most heartfelt birthday card I had ever received. I remember tears rolling down my face as I read every word.

For the first time in my life, I had heard the words that I had craved to hear as a little girl from my own father. I found out through that card that my dad really loved me and was very proud of who I was. He told me that he wouldn't change one thing about me and that he couldn't have asked for anything more. Those words helped me to lessen the fear I had towards him and it also helped me to let go of some horrible memories that some days still haunt me.

To be very honest, my dad and I still don't have a perfect relationship, and to be more honest, I don't know if we ever will. He still drives me insane due to his very strong personality. I know there are days when he still feels guilt and also days where my memories still cause me to hurt, but God is always faithful to remind me that forgiveness brings healing.

    I know it may not be the same for everyone. Maybe the person who hurt you is not sorry or maybe is still trying to hurt you. If that is the case, I would strongly urge you and plead with you to say something. You have to protect yourself. Don't let fear keep you from exposing that person. Remember, satan is manipulating them to hurt you. The sooner you get help, the sooner you let satan know that he does not have power over you. Trust that God will give you the strength.

GUILT

    Next, I want to talk about my guilty conscience. For such a long time I carried around a shame and a guilt that was so deeply sewn on my mind and soul. I, like many, know what it's like to feel blamed and responsible for being raped. I remember moments where I would just sit and think so hard on what it was that *I* had done wrong to deserve getting hurt by my dad. There must have been something I did wrong. Maybe if I had dressed differently or had a different body or maybe if I had acted differently or if I hadn't been so introverted and timid my dad would not have raped me. Would things have turned out another way if I had just been a little different? It just had to be my fault.

As a result, I was never able to feel comfortable in my own skin, but it was never as bad as when I would be around men. I always had a fear of being raped again by any man. It didn't matter who it was: my dad, my brothers, my father in law, friends, I still held that fear and guilt inside.

This was a very dark place for me. I took the blame for something that was never my fault. There finally came a point where God made it clear to me that He created me so specifically and perfectly that there was nothing about me that needed to be changed except for my thinking.

It breaks my heart to know that maybe you who are reading this and others out there across the world share that same feeling of guilt, but I'm here to inform you that God created every single ounce of who you are and who I am on purpose. Read the next passages and allow these words to seep into in your mind before you continue.

"For you created my inmost being; you knit me together in my mother's womb. I praise you because I am fearfully and wonderfully made; your works are wonderful, I know that full well. How precious to me are your thoughts, O God! How vast is the sum of them! Were I to count them, they would outnumber the grains of sand..."
- *Psalms 139:13-14, 17-18*

"Before I formed you in the womb I knew you, before you were born I set you apart..."
- *Jeremiah 1:5*

"...God created man in his own image, in the image of God he created him; male and female he created them."
- *Genesis 1:27*

Isn't it just amazing to know that the most high God created you in His own image in the most intricate and elaborate way just so that you would be who you are today? It amazes me every day to think that I am who I am on purpose. I'm not going to lie, I still have a fear of being alone with any man without my husband or someone else around, but I no longer blame myself for it. It's satan's fault and his fault alone. It is so important that you really take a hold of this truth. There is nothing like it. I can tell you from experience that the moment I really grasped that I wasn't responsible for what happened to me, I was truly able to let go of all the lies that satan had been feeding my soul. I was able to live again and really accept myself for who I am. There is nothing more that I want for you than that.

TELLING SOMEONE ELSE

Thirdly, I want to advise you to realize how vital it is for you to tell someone what you are going through or have gone through. Now, you don't want to go up to just anybody, because sometimes people can use really personal things against you or they may not be mature enough to handle it and advise you.

You should be very smart with whom you talk to. Perhaps a leader, a close friend that you trust, or a pastor would be a good person to talk to. The only person I ever told was my husband.

We had been dating for over a year and one night during worship at a youth service,

I felt the Lord press it on to my heart to tell him. I didn't want to at first, mainly because I was so scared of his reaction, but I could not and would not disobey God. A few days passed and I finally decided that it was time.

    I will always remember that night. I had called him and told him that I had something really important that I had to tell him. We went out for dinner and drove up to our favorite little stream. The sun had almost set and I remember my heart racing so fast I thought I would faint. I was extremely anxious and nervous and scared. I had NEVER told anyone, but God. I was very fidgety. I think I literally shifted positions every 2 seconds. I decided that I needed some air, so we got out of the car and walked down a path a little ways. Finally, after what felt like hours, I stopped and looked up at him, and through sobs and tears, I told him that someone had raped me. As I said those words that had been bottled up for years, it began to thunder and rain heavily. I cried harder and louder than ever before and after about 5 minutes I passed out.

    I remember waking up on a couch, not sure if I was just dreaming. Once I realized that it was not a dream, I began to cry. Not because I was hurting or embarrassed or anything like that, but because I felt liberated. I no longer held this secret that was a constant torment inside of me. I had finally released it. It was out in the open and it no longer had power over me.

Things may be very different for you, but even if it's not a secret, even if everyone around you knows that you were raped, molested, or what ever happened, you should never bottle up what you are feeling. It is never healthy. In my experience, even though God had rescued me from the hell I was living in, I never felt completely relieved of my big, dark secret until the moment I spoke up and told my husband. Even to this day, we have to talk about certain things that I am feeling because of bad memories that recur in my mind. I know now that if I bottle myself up and I don't let my husband know that something is bothering me, it takes a toll on me *and* my marriage. I find myself feeling ashamed again, and past emotions resurface.

That is why it's crucial for you to speak to somebody that you know you can trust. First, tell God what you are feeling. You can always talk to Him freely. *Then* tell someone whom you trust 100%. I think it's always important to talk to God and also a friend. God wants us to have people we can talk to about anything. It helps us so much, especially when we can't see past all the bad. If you don't have anyone you trust that knows God, pray that God will send you someone. Trust me, from someone who experienced it first hand, it is incredibly freeing.

SEXUAL INTIMACY

Lastly, I want to talk about sexual intimacy. But, before I begin, I really think it's important that you tell your current or future spouse your past beforehand, whatever it may be. Pray for the right words and the perfect timing. It will make the difference between a happy marriage and a painful one.

Sex was created and made to be this beautiful, culminating moment where a man and his wife are to consummate their love. It is meant to be one of the most romantic and breathtaking experiences for a couple. After being raped, I thought of sex as *the* most dirty, disgusting, sickening, and terrifying thing on earth. On my wedding night, I remember feeling so terrified, but I remember not wanting to expose my feelings. I felt cornered. I wanted to have a fun and romantic week like any bride, but all that I was feeling was fear. I was afraid of my husband getting mad at me if I told him that I was scared. I was worried that I would ruin our honeymoon if I didn't say anything because I was very uncomfortable and tense. So much fear was pent up inside of me, and I decided not to say anything *because*, in my mind, I would have put a strain on our relationship.

As a result, the first couple of days turned out to be painful and a little embarrassing for me. He knew something was wrong, but when he would ask me I would tell him that I was fine and that I was just tired. *Finally*, after about the millionth time that he asked me, I decided to tell him that I was scared. We were able to talk things out. I told him how I was feeling, both physically and emotionally, and I realized how ridiculous I was being to have not told him. He already knew everything that had happened in my past and he was very understanding. I should have known that he would have understood.

I'm not going to lie though, because even after we talked I still struggled with intimacy due to how painful it was and sometimes still is for me. Some days are better than others, but talking about it helped me to get through that week and through the first couple of months of marriage.

Now, I'm not saying sexual intimacy *will* be painful for you. Instead, I pray that it will be what you always dreamed it to be. What I am saying is that a lot of girls who *have* been sexually abused, unfortunately, suffer from pain during sex. I wish I could have had someone to talk to. *Had* someone told me what to expect in terms of sex after being raped, I think the first couple of days of my honeymoon wouldn't have been so uncomfortable. Unfortunately, I didn't have anyone, because nobody knew except for my husband. That is why I hope this helps you to get through your most fearful and uncomfortable moments.

I want to remind you that everyone is different and I know there will be some of you with certain things that affect *you* more than they will affect others. Maybe your experience was far more traumatic than mine. Maybe you were able to recover from your experience faster. Or maybe my struggles are a lot different from yours. But, no matter the differences, please remember that God loves you. He is always with you and you can always trust Him to bring you through your hardest moments. If you don't remember anything about this chapter, please remember that.

Chapter 7

Hope for Tomorrow

As I begin this chapter, I'm surrounded by the sounds of a loud dryer running and my 1 year old bumping his crib against the wall. I live the very busy and rewarding life of a full-time mom. I love it. Being a mom has brought such a different outlook on life for me. I never thought that an itty-bitty little being could change everything about someone. Even though God had turned my life around, it wasn't until I became a mommy that I could understand how big and intense the love for your child can be.

Believe it or not, it's not always rainbows and butterflies. Things can get pretty crazy in our day-to-day lives. I think my patience has been tested on a daily basis ever since the kids were born. Some days it takes a lot out of me to be nice and gentle when all I want to do is scream in frustration.

I consider the job of mothering the most bi-polar, draining, emotionally consuming, difficult job ever created by God, which leads me to say that I have come to the conclusion that God really does have an impeccable sense of humor. My mom was visiting the other day, and she couldn't help but laugh at how similar I was, as a baby, to my now 1-year-old little guy. Apparently, I drove my mom up the wall as a baby and yet, I turned out to be a very calm, quiet, and shy person. How that happened, I don't know. It *must* be God's impeccable sense of humor. I just hope my son follows my lead and calms down at least a little. I keep praying and asking God to direct my parenting and also to help me to grow through the process of raising two little men who love and trust Him. My hope is to able to look back when they are a lot older and know that I did my best as a mother.

In addition to mothering I am also a wife. I want to be very honest and say that I struggle with being the wife I want to be. I have the most amazing husband in the world. He truly is a Super Man. He does everything for my boys and me. I don't know where I'd be without him and yet, I have a hard time loving him the way he should be loved. Some days I look at other wives and envy the patience and respect they have towards their husbands, and I can't figure out why it is that I am not that way towards this amazing man that God put in my life. I have told him this many times and never once has he agreed with me. He has seen me at my worst, and even in my ugliest moments, and yet, I am still amazed at how much grace and love he shows me. My husband has unveiled God's true, unconditional love to me, and for that I am eternally grateful. If I could be half the person he is, I would be happy.

I'm not content at where I stand today as a wife and companion to my husband, but God has done a lot of work in me up till now, and I pray that he would continue to mold me into the wife He has called me to be to my hero.

It has been quite an adventure writing this book. I've had my ups and downs, felt really excited at times and then also really sad. I think that the hardest part of this entire process, for me, has been that I haven't been able to tell my closest friends about it. My mom and siblings still have no clue about anything. The days when I felt really excited because God put something in my heart to write, I just wanted to call them up to celebrate. Then there were those moments when all I wanted was to cry with my mom just so she could hold me and tell me that everything was going to work out great.

It still pains me that I will never be able to celebrate this with them, but I can't help but think of all the untainted memories they will have of us as a family. I know that it's better this way for everyone. I never want my mom or my siblings to see my dad as a father that raped his daughter because he is no longer that person. Today my dad is a hardworking man who loves his family and can't help but melt at the sight of all his grandchildren.

I want my family to remember all the good memories we had: the days when we go to a nearby park to play sports together as kids, the fun road trips we would take where my dad would always find places with the most beautiful scenery, and the unforgettable days when we would spontaneously end up at a carnival or ice cream shop just because. Those are memories that I want them to remember because those are the memories that now stand out in my mind.

God has been so faithful to both my family and me. It is still crazy to me how He can really take a hold of someone's life and turn it all around. I was like a wounded bird that couldn't fly, but God healed me and gave me the strength to soar higher than I could have ever imagined. Had I ever been told, before writing this book, that I would have the chance to tell the world my testimony, I wouldn't have even given it another thought. But, with God guiding me every step of the way, I've accomplished so much more than I thought could even be possible. Words can't express how grateful I am for all He has done for my family and me.

Tomorrow is a chance for new memories, *good* memories, and there's nothing more that I want than to be able to share those great memories with my family: God, my husband, my babies, my siblings, my mom, AND yes, my dad.

www.ingramcontent.com/pod-product-compliance
Ingram Content Group UK Ltd.
Pitfield, Milton Keynes, MK11 3LW, UK
UKHW041949230426
12048UKWH00008B/219